Eucharistic Prayers for Concelebration

ANDREAS
PETRVS

Eucharistic Prayers for Concelebration

**Includes all Ten Eucharistic Prayers
Approved for Use
in the Dioceses of the United States of America
by the United States Conference of Catholic Bishops
and Confirmed by the Apostolic See**

**ENGLISH TRANSLATION ACCORDING
TO THE THIRD TYPICAL EDITION
OF THE ROMAN MISSAL**

CATHOLIC BOOK PUBLISHING CORP.
New Jersey

Published by authority of the Committee on Divine Worship,
United States Conference of Catholic Bishops

(T-24)

ISBN 978-0-89942-544-3

Printed in U.S.A.
catholicbookpublishing.com

CONTENTS

From the
GENERAL INSTRUCTION OF THE ROMAN MISSAL

199. Concelebration, by which the unity of the Priesthood, of the Sacrifice, and also of the whole People of God is appropriately expressed, is prescribed by the rite itself for the Ordination of a Bishop and of Priests, at the Blessing of an Abbot, and at the Chrism Mass.

205. A concelebrated Mass, whatever its form, is arranged in accordance with the norms commonly in force (cf. nos. 112–198), observing or adapting however what is set out below.

THE EUCHARISTIC PRAYER

78. Now the center and high point of the entire celebration begins, namely, the Eucharistic Prayer itself, that is, the prayer of thanksgiving and sanctification. The Priest calls upon the people to lift up their hearts towards the Lord in prayer and thanksgiving; he associates the people with himself in the Prayer that he addresses in the name of the entire community to God the Father through Jesus Christ in the Holy Spirit. Furthermore, the meaning of this Prayer is that the whole congregation of the faithful joins with Christ in confessing the great deeds of God and in the offering of Sacrifice. The Eucharistic Prayer requires that everybody listens to it with reverence and in silence.

79. The main elements of which the Eucharistic Prayer consists may be distinguished from one another in this way:

a) The *thanksgiving* (expressed especially in the Preface), in which the Priest, in the name of the whole of the holy people, glorifies God the Father and gives thanks to him for the whole work of salvation or for some particular aspect of it, according to the varying day, festivity, or time of year.

b) The *acclamation*, by which the whole congregation, joining with the heavenly powers, sings the *Sanctus* (*Holy, Holy, Holy*). This acclamation, which constitutes part of the Eucharistic Prayer itself, is pronounced by all the people with the Priest.

c) The *epiclesis*, in which, by means of particular invocations, the Church implores the power of the Holy Spirit that the gifts offered by human hands be consecrated, that is, become Christ's Body and Blood, and that the unblemished sacrificial Victim to be consumed in Communion may be for the salvation of those who will partake of it.

d) The *Institution narrative and Consecration*, by which, by means of the words and actions of Christ, that Sacrifice is effected which Christ himself instituted during the Last Supper, when he offered his Body and Blood under the species of bread and wine, gave them to the Apostles to eat and drink, and leaving with the latter the command to perpetuate this same mystery.

e) The *anamnesis*, by which the Church, fulfilling the command that she received from Christ the Lord through the Apostles, celebrates the memorial of Christ, recalling especially his blessed Passion, glorious Resurrection and Ascension into heaven.

f) The *oblation*, by which, in this very memorial, the Church, in particular that gathered here and now, offers the unblemished sacrificial Victim in the Holy Spirit to the Father. The Church's intention, indeed, is that the faithful not only offer this unblemished sacrificial Victim but also learn to offer their very selves, and so day by day to be brought, through the mediation of Christ, into unity with God and with each other, so that God may at last be all in all.

g) The *intercessions*, by which expression is given to the fact that the Eucharist is celebrated in communion with the whole Church, of both heaven and of earth, and that the oblation is made for her and for all her members, living and dead, who are called to participate in the redemption and salvation purchased by the Body and Blood of Christ.

h) The *concluding doxology*, by which the glorification of God is expressed and which is affirmed and concluded by the people's acclamation *Amen*.

[THE MANNER OF RECITING THE EUCHARISTIC PRAYER]

148. As he begins the Eucharistic Prayer, the Priest extends his hands and sings or says, *The Lord be with you.* The people reply, *And with your spirit.* As he continues, saying, *Lift up your hearts,* he raises his hands. The people reply, *We lift them up to the Lord.* Then the Priest, with hands extended, adds, *Let us give thanks to the Lord our God,* and the people reply, *It is right and just.* After this, the Priest, with hands extended, continues the Preface. At its conclusion, he joins his hands and, together with all those present, sings or says aloud the *Sanctus (Holy, Holy, Holy)* (cf. no. 79 b).

149. The Priest continues the Eucharistic Prayer in accordance with the rubrics that are set out in each of the Prayers.

If the celebrant is a Bishop, in the Prayers, after the words *N., our Pope,* he adds, *and me, your unworthy servant.* If, however, the Bishop is celebrating outside his own diocese, after the words *with . . . N., our Pope,* he adds, *my brother N., the Bishop of this Church, and me, your unworthy servant;* or after the words *especially . . . N., our Pope,* he adds, *my brother N., the Bishop of this Church, and me, your unworthy servant.*

The Diocesan Bishop, or one who is equivalent to the Diocesan Bishop in law, must be mentioned by means of this formula: *together with your servant N., our Pope, and N., our Bishop* (or *Vicar, Prelate, Prefect, Abbot*).

It is permitted to mention Coadjutor Bishop and Auxiliary Bishops in the Eucharistic Prayer, but not other Bishops who happen to be present. When several are to be mentioned, this is done with the collective formula: *N., our Bishop and his assistant Bishops.*

In each of the Eucharistic Prayers, these formulas are to be adapted according to the requirements of grammar.

150. A little before the Consecration, if appropriate, a minister rings a small bell as a signal to the faithful. The minister also rings the small bell at each elevation by the Priest, according to local custom.

If incense is being used, when the host and the chalice are shown to the people after the Consecration, a minister incenses them.

THE MANNER OF PRONOUNCING THE EUCHARISTIC PRAYER

216. The Preface is sung or said by the principal Priest Celebrant alone; but the *Sanctus (Holy, Holy, Holy)* is sung or recited by all the concelebrants, together with the people and the choir.

217. After the *Sanctus (Holy, Holy, Holy)*, the concelebrating Priests continue the Eucharistic Prayer in the way described below. Only the principal celebrant makes the gestures, unless other indications are given.

218. The parts pronounced by all the concelebrants together and especially the words of Consecration, which all are obliged to say, are to be recited in such a manner that the concelebrants speak them in a low voice and that the principal celebrant's voice is heard clearly. In this way the words can be more easily understood by the people.

It is a praiseworthy practice for the parts that are to be said by all the concelebrants together and for which musical notation is provided in the Missal to be sung.

Eucharistic Prayer I, or the Roman Canon

219. In Eucharistic Prayer I, or the Roman Canon, the *Te igitur (To you, therefore, most merciful Father)* is said by the principal celebrant alone, with hands extended.

220. It is appropriate that the commemoration *(Memento)* of the living and the *Communicantes (In communion with those)* be assigned to one or other of the concelebrating Priests, who then pronounces these prayers alone, with hands extended, and in a loud voice.

221. The *Hanc igitur (Therefore, Lord, we pray)* is said once again by the principal celebrant alone, with hands extended.

222. From the *Quam oblationem (Be pleased, O God, we pray)* up to and including the *Supplices (In humble prayer we ask you, almighty God)*, the

principal celebrant alone makes the gestures, while all the concelebrants pronounce everything together, in this manner:

a) the *Quam oblationem (Be pleased, O God, we pray)*, with hands extended toward the offerings;

b) the *Qui pridie (On the day before he was to suffer)* and the *Simili modo (In a similar way)* with hands joined;

c) the words of the Lord, with each extending his right hand toward the bread and toward the chalice, if this seems appropriate; and at the elevation looking toward them and after this bowing profoundly;

d) the *Unde et memores (Therefore, O Lord, as we celebrate the memorial)* and the *Supra quae (Be pleased to look upon)* with hands extended;

e) for the *Supplices (In humble prayer we ask you, almighty God)* up to and including the words *through this participation at the altar,* bowing with hands joined; then standing upright and crossing themselves at the words *may be filled with every grace and heavenly blessing.*

223. It is appropriate that the commemoration (*Memento*) of the dead and the *Nobis quoque peccatoribus (To us, also, your servants)* be assigned to one or other of the concelebrants, who pronounces them alone, with hands extended, and in a loud voice.

224. At the words *To us, also, your servants, who though sinners,* of the *Nobis quoque peccatoribus,* all the concelebrants strike their breast.

225. The *Per quem haec omnia (Through whom you continue)* is said by the principal celebrant alone.

Eucharistic Prayer II

226. In Eucharistic Prayer II, the part *You are indeed Holy, O Lord* is pronounced by the principal celebrant alone, with hands extended.

227. In the parts from *Make holy, therefore, these gifts* to the end of *Humbly we pray,* all the concelebrants pronounce everything together as follows:

a) the part *Make holy, therefore, these gifts,* with hands extended toward the offerings;

b) the parts *At the time he was betrayed* and *In a similar way* with hands joined;

c) the words of the Lord, with each extending his right hand toward the bread and toward the chalice, if this seems appropriate; and at the elevation looking toward them and after this bowing profoundly;

d) the parts *Therefore, as we celebrate* and *Humbly we pray* with hands extended.

228. It is appropriate that the intercessions for the living, *Remember, Lord, your Church,* and for the dead, *Remember also our brothers and sisters,* be

assigned to one or other of the concelebrants, who pronounces them alone, with hands extended, and in a loud voice.

Eucharistic Prayer III

229. In Eucharistic Prayer III, the part *You are indeed Holy, O Lord* is pronounced by the principal celebrant alone, with hands extended.

230. In the parts from *Therefore, O Lord, we humbly implore you* to the end of *Look, we pray upon the oblation,* all the concelebrants pronounce everything together as follows:

a) the part *Therefore, O Lord, we humbly implore you* with hands extended toward the offerings;

b) the parts *For on the night he was betrayed* and *In a similar way* with hands joined;

c) the words of the Lord, with each extending his right hand toward the bread and toward the chalice, if this seems appropriate; and at the elevation looking toward them and after this bowing profoundly;

d) the parts *Therefore, O Lord, as we celebrate the memorial* and *Look, we pray, upon the oblation* with hands extended.

231. It is appropriate that the intercessions *May he make of us an eternal offering to you,* and *May this Sacrifice of our reconciliation,* and *To our departed brothers and sisters* be assigned to one or other of the concelebrants, who pronounces them alone, with hands extended, and in a loud voice.

Eucharistic Prayer IV

232. In Eucharistic Prayer IV, the part *We give you praise, Father most holy* up to and including the words *he might sanctify creation to the full* is pronounced by the principal celebrant alone, with hands extended.

233. In the parts from *Therefore, O Lord, we pray* to the end of *Look, O Lord, upon the Sacrifice,* all the concelebrants pronounce everything together as follows:

a) the part *Therefore, O Lord, we pray* with hands extended toward the offerings;

b) the parts *For when the hour had come* and *In a similar way* with hands joined;

c) the words of the Lord, with each extending his right hand toward the bread and toward the chalice, if this seems appropriate; and at the elevation looking toward them and after this bowing profoundly;

d) the parts *Therefore, O Lord, as we now celebrate* and *Look, O Lord, upon the Sacrifice* with hands extended.

234. It is appropriate that the intercessions *Therefore, Lord, remember now* and *To all of us, your children* be assigned to one or other of the concelebrants, who pronounces them alone, with hands extended, and in a loud voice.

235. As for other Eucharistic Prayers approved by the Apostolic See, the norms laid down for each one are to be observed.

236. The concluding doxology of the Eucharistic Prayer is pronounced solely by the principal Priest Celebrant or together, if this is desired, with the other concelebrants, but not by the faithful.

From *THE ROMAN MISSAL*

EUCHARISTIC PRAYERS FOR RECONCILIATION

[For concelebration, these Eucharistic Prayers are said in the following way:]

Eucharistic Prayer for Reconciliation I

The Preface and *You are indeed Holy, O Lord* to *just as you yourself are holy* inclusive are said by the principal celebrant alone, with hands extended.

From *Look, we pray* to *we, too, are your sons and daughters* inclusive is said together by all the concelebrants, with hands extended toward the offerings.

From *But before* to *who heals every division* inclusive, all the concelebrants together speak in this manner:

a) The part *But before*, with hands joined.

b) While speaking the words of the Lord, each extends his right hand toward the bread and toward the chalice, if this seems appropriate; as the host and the chalice are elevated at the Consecration, however, the concelebrants look toward them and then bow profoundly.

c) The parts *Therefore, as we celebrate the memorial* and *Look kindly, most compassionate Father*, with hands extended.

It is appropriate that the intercession *Be pleased to keep us always in communion of mind and heart* be assigned to one or other of the concelebrants, who pronounces this prayer alone, with hands extended.

The following parts especially may be sung: *But before*; *As he ate with them*; *In a similar way*; *Therefore, as we celebrate the memorial*; *Look kindly, most compassionate Father*, as well as the concluding doxology.

The concluding doxology of the Eucharistic Prayer is pronounced by the principal celebrant alone, or by all the concelebrants together with the principal celebrant.

Eucharistic Prayer for Reconciliation II

The Preface and *You, therefore, almighty Father* to *handed over to death* inclusive are said by the principal celebrant alone, with hands extended.

From *And now, celebrating the reconciliation* to *when we celebrate these mysteries* inclusive is spoken together by all the concelebrants, with hands extended toward the offerings.

From *For when about to give his life* to *the Sacrifice of perfect reconciliation* inclusive, all the concelebrants together speak in this manner:

a) The part *For when about to give his life*, with hands joined.

b) While speaking the words of the Lord, each extends his right hand toward the bread and toward the chalice, if this seems appropriate; as the host and the chalice are elevated at the Consecration, however, the concelebrants look toward them and then bow profoundly.

c) The part *Celebrating therefore the memorial*, with hands extended.

It is appropriate that the intercessions *May he make your Church* and *Just as you have gathered us now* be assigned to one or other of the concelebrants, who pronounces this prayer alone, with hands extended.

The following parts especially may be sung: *And now, celebrating the reconciliation*; *For when about to give his life*; *In a similar way on that same evening*; *Celebrating therefore the memorial*, as well as the concluding doxology.

The concluding doxology of the Eucharistic Prayer is pronounced by the principal celebrant alone, or by all the concelebrants together with the principal celebrant.

EUCHARISTIC PRAYERS FOR VARIOUS NEEDS

The Preface and *You are indeed Holy* to *and breaks the bread* inclusive are said by the principal celebrant alone, with hands extended.

From *Therefore, Father most merciful* to *of our Lord Jesus Christ* inclusive is spoken together by all the concelebrants, with hands extended toward the offerings.

From *On the day before he was to suffer* to *in whose Body and Blood we have communion* inclusive, all the concelebrants together speak in this manner:

a) The part *On the day before he was to suffer*, with hands joined.

b) While speaking the words of the Lord, each extends his right hand toward the bread and toward the chalice, if this seems appropriate; as the host and the chalice are elevated at the Consecration, however, the concelebrants look toward them and then bow profoundly.

c) The parts *Therefore, holy Father* and *Look with favor on the oblation of your Church*, with hands extended.

It is appropriate that the intercessions *Lord, renew your Church*; or *And so, having called us to your table*; or *By our partaking*; or *Bring your Church, O Lord*; as well as *Remember our brothers and sisters*; be assigned to one or other of the concelebrants, who pronounces these prayers alone, with hands extended.

The following parts especially may be sung: *On the day before he was to suffer*; *In a similar way*; *Therefore, holy Father*; *Look with favor on the oblation of your Church*, as well as the concluding doxology.

The concluding doxology of the Eucharistic Prayer is pronounced by the principal celebrant alone, or by all the concelebrants along with the principal celebrant.

GUIDELINES FOR CONCELEBRATION OF THE EUCHARIST

The document Guidelines for Concelebration of the Eucharist *was developed by the Bishops' Committee on the Liturgy of the United States Conference of Catholic Bishops (USCCB). It was approved by the full body of bishops at its November 2003 General Meeting and has been authorized for publication by the undersigned.*

Msgr. William P. Fay
General Secretary, USCCB

INTRODUCTION

1. Concelebration is the practice by which "several priests, in virtue of Christ's own Priesthood and in the person of the High Priest, act together with one voice and one will; so also do they confect and offer a single sacrifice by a single sacramental act and likewise partake of the same."[1]
2. The Fathers of the Second Vatican Council recommended concelebration as an expression of "the unity of the priesthood"[2] and chose to extend permission for the practice to a number of particular instances, granting the Bishop of each diocese the authority to decide when concelebration was opportune at other times. The Council further directed that "a new rite for concelebration . . . be drawn up and inserted into the *Pontifical* and into the *Roman Missal*."[3]
3. On March 7, 1965, the Council's directives were fulfilled in the publication of the Decree *Ecclesiae semper* and the accompanying *Rite of Concelebration*. From the earliest days of the Church, concelebration, while taking a variety of forms, has been celebrated for "much more than merely practical considerations."[4] For such concelebration at Mass is expressive of the one sacrifice of the cross, the priesthood, and the action of the entire People of God, "ordered and acting hierarchically."[5] Concelebration should be understood as an appropriate way for priests

[1] Sacred Congregation of Rites, *Ecclesiae Semper* (ES), March 7, 1965: AAS 57 (1965), 410-412.

[2] See Second Vatican Council, *Sacrosanctum Concilium* (SC), December 4, 1963, no. 57 §1, 2a: "at conventual Mass, and at the principal Mass in churches when the needs of the faithful do not require that all priests available should celebrate individually and at Masses celebrated at any kind of priests' meetings, whether the priests be secular clergy or religious," and SC, 57 §1, 1: (a) on the Thursday of the Lord's Supper, not only at the Mass of the Chrism, but also at the evening Mass; (b) at Masses during councils, Bishops' conferences, and synods; (c) at the Mass for the blessing of an abbot.

[3] SC, no. 58.

[4] ES.

[5] ES.

to participate in the celebration of the Eucharist, expressive of their unique relationship with Christ the High Priest and of the unity of the priesthood.

GENERAL PRINCIPLES

Regulation of Concelebration

4. The purpose of these guidelines is to provide a summary of the Church's practice in regard to Eucharistic concelebration. They do not constitute new liturgical law, but enjoy the authority of the law cited. These guidelines may be adapted by diocesan Bishops within the parameters of liturgical law. This document is limited to questions directly pertaining to Eucharistic concelebration.
5. The regulation of concelebration belongs to the diocesan Bishop, who may establish diocesan guidelines regarding concelebration.[6] "Every Priest, however, is allowed to celebrate the Eucharist individually, though not at the same time as a concelebration is taking place in the same church or oratory. However, on Holy Thursday, and for the Mass of the Easter Vigil, it is not permitted to celebrate Mass individually."[7]

Participation in Concelebration

6. "[Priests] 'as ministers of holy things, above all in the Sacrifice of the Mass, act especially in the person of Christ' (*Presbyterorum Ordinis*, no. 13, see also *Lumen Gentium*, no. 28). Hence it is fitting that, because of the sign value *(ratione signi)*, priests should participate in the Eucharist, fulfilling their office according to their proper order, that is by celebrating Mass rather than merely receiving communion as lay persons."[8]
7. Therefore, concelebration is always encouraged, "unless the welfare of the Christian faithful requires or urges otherwise."[9] "Visiting Priests should be gladly admitted to concelebration of the Eucharist, provided their Priestly standing has been ascertained,"[10] and "a superior may not prohibit a priest from concelebrating,"[11] except in the instances described in no. 10, below.

---

[6] See *General Instruction of the Roman Missal, third typical edition* (GIRM), April 20, 2000, no. 202.

[7] GIRM, no. 199; see SC, 57 §2.

[8] Sacred Congregation of Rites, *Eucharisticum Mysterium* (EM), May 25, 1967, no. 43.

[9] *Code of Canon Law*, Canon 902: "Priests may concelebrate the Eucharist unless the welfare of the Christian faithful requires or urges otherwise but with due regard for the freedom of each priest to celebrate the Eucharist individually, though not during the time when there is a concelebration in the same church or oratory."

[10] GIRM, no. 200.

[11] In a *responsum ad dubium*, dated July 3, 1999 (Prot. 1411/99), the Congregation for Divine Worship and the Discipline of the Sacraments has reinforced the freedom of all priests to concelebrate. No superior may prohibit a priest from concelebrating. The response also notes that "it is laudable that [priests enjoying the faculty of celebrating Mass in the rite in force before the liturgical renewal of Vatican Council II] concelebrate freely especially for the Mass of the Thursday of Holy Week, with the diocesan Bishop presiding. . . . The sign of communion inherent in concelebration is so particular that it ought not to be omitted in the Chrism Mass except for grave reasons."

8. Concelebration is "prescribed by the rite itself for the Ordination of a Bishop and of Priests, at the Blessing of an Abbot, and at the Chrism Mass"[12] because it appropriately expresses "the unity of the Priesthood, of the Sacrifice, and also of the whole People of God."[13] Concelebration is also recommended at the evening Mass on Holy Thursday, the Mass for councils, meetings of Bishops, synods, the conventual Mass, the principal Mass in churches and oratories, and the Mass for any kind of meeting of priests, either secular or religious.[14]
9. "In a eucharistic celebration presided over by the bishop, presbyters should concelebrate with him so that the mystery of the unity of the Church may be made manifest through the eucharistic celebration and so that the presbyters may be seen by the entire community to be the presbyterate of the bishop."[15]
10. "No one is ever to join a concelebration or to be admitted as a concelebrant once the Mass has already begun."[16]

Number of Concelebrants

11. Each Ordinary or the Major Superior of clerical non-exempt religious and of societies of clerics living in common[17] may limit the number of concelebrants if, in consideration of the size of the church and the altar and whether the faithful's view of the rite is impaired, he decides "that the dignity of the rite requires this."[18]
12. In those instances where it is advisable to limit the number of concelebrants, the priests chosen to concelebrate should be truly representative of the larger group. Such a limitation on the number of concelebrants should be understood as a pastoral response to the problems of space which may occur because of the great number of priests who may be present rather than as an attempt at exclusion.
13. In those cases when the number of concelebrants is limited for legitimate reasons, those in charge of planning should provide opportunities for the non-concelebrating priests to celebrate the Eucharist at another time.

Physical Arrangements

14. Concelebrants should be seated together in a distinct area (*presbyterium*). They should not be intermingled with the assembly nor should anyone be seated between the concelebrants and the altar. If the space in the *presbyterium* is not large enough to accommodate all the concelebrants appropriately, some are seated in another area which physically and visually unites them with the other concelebrants.

---

[12] GIRM, no. 199.

[13] GIRM, no. 199.

[14] See GIRM, no. 199.

[15] *Caeremoniale Episcoporum* (CE), September 14, 1984, no. 21.

[16] GIRM, no. 206.

[17] See GIRM, no. 202: "It is for the Bishop, in accordance with the norm of law, to regulate the discipline for concelebration in all churches and oratories of his diocese."

[18] Sacred Congregation of Rites, *Rite of Concelebration* (RC), March 7, 1965, nos. 3 and 4.

15. The position of the concelebrants should not obscure the fact that only one Bishop or one priest presides over the whole celebration. Furthermore, the position of the concelebrants should not usurp the positions or limit the functioning of other liturgical ministers. Unless it is unavoidable, concelebrants should not impede the full view of the assembly, since members of the congregation are called upon to kneel at various times during Mass.[19]

Vesture

16. "In the Church, which is the Body of Christ, not all members have the same function. This diversity of offices is shown outwardly in the celebration of the Eucharist by the diversity of sacred vestments, which must therefore be a sign of the function proper to each minister. Moreover, these same sacred vestments should also contribute to the decoration of the sacred action itself."[20]

17. Concelebrating priests wear an alb with a stole and chasuble. However, if "a just cause arise[s] (e.g., a more considerable number of concelebrants or a lack of vestments), concelebrants other than the principal celebrant may omit the chasuble and simply wear the stole over the alb."[21]

18. The principal celebrant is to wear the alb with a stole and chasuble.[22]

19. Priests may not concelebrate in secular attire, in ordinary clerical garb, or by wearing the stole over the cassock. Nor may priests of religious institutes concelebrate merely by placing a stole over the monastic cowl or habit.[23]

20. If chasubles are worn by all the concelebrants, they should be simpler in their decoration than that of the principal celebrant. Vestments that differ in size, shape, and ornamentation can obscure unity, emphasize individualism, and detract from the presidential role of the principal celebrant. The vestments of the concelebrants should be of the color proper to the Mass being celebrated. "However, the proper color being kept by the principal celebrant, the concelebrants may in case of necessity use white. . . ."[24]

RITE OF CONCELEBRATION

Reverence to the Altar

21. Concelebrants should participate in the entrance or recessional chant or maintain a reverential silence. The principal celebrant and deacon(s), together with concelebrants and other ministers in the procession, bow to the altar on arrival as a sign of reverence. "If, however, the tabernacle

[19] See GIRM, no. 43.
[20] GIRM, no. 335.
[21] GIRM, no. 209.
[22] See GIRM, no. 209.
[23] See Sacred Congregation for Divine Worship, *Liturgicae Instaurationes*, September 5, 1970, no. 8c.
[24] See RC, no. 12.

with the Most Blessed Sacrament is present in the sanctuary, the priest, the deacon, and the other ministers [including concelebrants] genuflect when they approach the altar and when they depart from it, but not during the celebration of Mass itself."[25] The principal celebrant, the deacon(s), and any concelebrants then venerate the altar with a kiss.[26]

The Gospel

22. When there is no deacon present, a concelebrant proclaims the Gospel.[27] If the principal celebrant is a Bishop, the concelebrant asks for and receives a blessing from the Bishop, and proclaims the gospel reading in the usual way.[28] If the principal celebrant is not a Bishop, the concelebrant bows before the altar and prays inaudibly, *Cleanse my heart and my lips, almighty God*, and proclaims the gospel reading in the usual way.[29] After the proclamation of the Gospel, if the *Book of the Gospels* is brought to the Bishop, the concelebrants remain standing.

The Homily

23. The homily is usually given by the principal celebrant or, at his invitation, by one of the concelebrants,[30] or even, in some cases, by a deacon.[31]

Preparation of the Altar and the Gifts

24. "The Preparation of the Gifts (cf. nos. 139-146) is carried out by the principal celebrant, while the other concelebrants remain at their places."[32] When there are to be great numbers of communicants and all the ciboria cannot conveniently be placed on the altar, some of the concelebrants may hold the ciboria in their hands during the Eucharistic Prayer.

At the Altar

25. The concelebrants approach the altar for the Eucharistic Prayer after the principal celebrant has concluded the prayer over the offerings. If there is a great number of concelebrants, only some of them should be invited to stand with the principal celebrant at the altar. The deacons remain "behind the concelebrants, but in such a way that one of them may assist at the cup and the book as needed."[33] The Eucharistic Prayer should be chosen prior to the celebration. The principal celebrant begins the Eucharistic Prayer only after the concelebrants have taken their places.

---

[25] See GIRM, no. 274.

[26] See GIRM, no. 211.

[27] See GIRM, no. 212; see *Book of the Gospels* (BG), no. 14.

[28] See BG, no. 15.

[29] *Lectionary for Mass for Use in the Dioceses of the United States of America* (LFM), November 29, 1998, no. 17.

[30] See GIRM, no. 213.

[31] See GIRM, no. 66.

[32] GIRM, no. 214.

[33] CE, no. 153; see GIRM, no. 215.

Singing of the Eucharistic Prayer

26. It is very appropriate that the principal celebrant sing those parts of the Eucharistic Prayer for which musical notation in the *Missal* is provided and that concelebrants sing together the parts assigned to them.[34] However, the Eucharistic Prayer should not be sung unless the principal celebrant and the concelebrants know the music and are able to sing it well.

Proclamation of the Eucharistic Prayer

27. When it is not sung, the Eucharistic Prayer should be proclaimed by the principal celebrant in a loud and clear voice. Concelebrating priests recite the epiclesis, words of consecration, anamnesis, and post-consecratory epiclesis in a very low voice, so that the congregation is able to hear the text without difficulty.[35] The concelebrants listen in silence during the post-Sanctus and the intercessions.

Deacons and Other Ministers

28. When neither a deacon nor other ministers assist in a concelebrated Mass, their functions are to be carried out by one or more of the concelebrants.[36] However, every effort should be made to provide a deacon and other ministers.

Epiclesis

29. In accord with ancient tradition, concelebrating priests stretch out both their hands toward the elements during the epiclesis.[37] The full impact of this gesture can be achieved if the concelebrants adopt the same gesture as the principal celebrant.

Consecration

30. During the consecration, each concelebrant extends the right hand toward the bread and the chalice.[38]
31. All bow profoundly when the principal celebrant genuflects after the consecration of the bread and after the consecration of the wine.

Anamnesis and Epiclesis

32. The concelebrants hold their hands outstretched in an *orans* gesture during the anamnesis and the post-consecratory epiclesis, but not during the other parts of the Eucharistic Prayer.

Additional Gestures in the Roman Canon

33. When praying the First Eucharistic Prayer (Roman Canon), concelebrants make two additional gestures. From *In humble prayer we ask you, almighty God* to *the most holy Body and Blood of your Son* inclu-

---

[34] See GIRM, nos. 147, 218.
[35] See GIRM, no. 218.
[36] See GIRM, no. 208.
[37] See GIRM, nos. 222a, 227a, 230a, 233a.
[38] See GIRM, nos. 222c, 227c, 230c, 233c.

sive, they bow with hands joined; then they stand upright and cross themselves at the words *may be filled.*[39] At the words *To us, also, your servants, who, though sinners*, each concelebrant strikes his breast.[40]

The Intercessions

34. If they are to be prayed by designated concelebrants, the intercessions within the Eucharistic Prayer should be assigned prior to the beginning of the celebration. Cards or booklets containing the Eucharistic Prayer should be provided to those concelebrants who will read one or more of the intercessions. In this way, the passing of the *Missal* on the altar from one concelebrant to another will be avoided.

35. Each individual concelebrant chosen to pray the intercessions does so with his hands extended. Careful attention should be given to the manner in which the intercessions are divided.[41] The principal celebrant may also say the intercessions by himself.

Doxology of the Eucharistic Prayer

36. During the final doxology of the Eucharistic Prayer only the principal celebrant elevates the paten with the consecrated bread, while the deacon raises the chalice. The concelebrants do not elevate other chalices, ciboria, or other sacred vessels. If no deacon is present, one of the concelebrants may elevate the chalice.

37. All the concelebrants may join in the singing or recitation of the doxology if this is desirable or it may be sung or recited by the principal celebrant alone.[42] *The collective voice of the concelebrants should not, however, overwhelm the voice of the principal celebrant.* The procedure to be followed should be decided by the principal celebrant before the celebration begins.

The Lord's Prayer

38. "Then the principal celebrant, with hands joined, says the introduction to the Lord's Prayer. Next, with hands extended, he says the Lord's Prayer itself together with the other concelebrants, who also pray with hands extended, and together with the people."[43] Only the principal celebrant maintains the *orans* posture for the *Deliver us, Lord, we pray, from every evil. . . .*

Prayers During the Communion Rite

39. The celebrant's parts of the Communion Rite are said by the principal celebrant alone. They may not be distributed for recitation by the concelebrants. Nor may they be recited by the concelebrants together with the principal celebrant.[44]

---

[39] See GIRM, no. 222e.

[40] See GIRM, no. 224.

[41] See GIRM, nos. 216-236.

[42] See GIRM, no. 236.

[43] GIRM, no. 237; see CE, no. 159.

[44] See GIRM, nos. 238, 241.

Sign of Peace

40. The sign of peace should not be overextended, thus delaying the rite of the breaking of the consecrated bread.[45]

Breaking of the Bread

41. The Lamb of God begins only after the sign of peace is completed. During this litany the deacon (or, in his absence, one or more of the concelebrants) assists the principal celebrant in the breaking of the consecrated bread.[46]
42. It is not necessary that each concelebrant receive one-half of a large host. But at least some of the Eucharistic bread should be broken for the concelebrants and the people.
43. It is strongly recommended that the faithful receive the Lord's Body from the bread consecrated at the same Mass.[47] Concelebrants must never be given Holy Communion consecrated at another Mass and reserved in the tabernacle, and they are to receive under both species.[48]
44. The concelebrants can receive hosts in two ways. When the principal celebrant's private prayer before Communion is finished, the principal celebrant genuflects and steps back a little. One after another, the concelebrants come to the middle of the altar, genuflect, and reverently take the Body of Christ from the altar. Then, holding the Eucharistic bread in one hand, with the other hand under it, they return to their places. Alternately, the concelebrants may remain in their places and take the Body of Christ from the paten presented to them by the principal celebrant, or by one or more of the concelebrants or deacons, or also from the paten as it is passed from one to another.[49] The formula *The Body of Christ* is not said.
45. When sufficient concelebrants are present, they assist the principal celebrant in the distribution of Holy Communion. When the number of ordinary ministers of Holy Communion is insufficient, extraordinary ministers of Holy Communion may assist in the distribution of the Eucharist. Such extraordinary ministers do not receive Holy Communion in the manner of concelebrants. Rather, they receive the Body and Blood of the Lord after the principal celebrant and the deacon.

Invitation to Holy Communion

46. Only the principal celebrant shows the consecrated host to the people when he proclaims, *Behold the Lamb of God.*[50] Concelebrants do not elevate their hosts; rather, they reverently hold the consecrated bread in the right hand with the left hand under it.

[45] See GIRM, no. 154.

[46] See GIRM, no. 240.

[47] See SC, no. 55; GIRM, no. 85; EM, no. 31.

[48] For an exception, see the circular letter of the Congregation for Doctrine of the Faith dated July 24, 2003 (Prot. 89/78-17498), no. B3.

[49] See GIRM, no. 242.

[50] See GIRM, no. 243.

Receiving the Body of the Lord

47. After the invitation to Communion, the principal celebrant alone says in a lower voice, *May the Body of Christ keep me safe for eternal life.* He then consumes the Body of Christ. If the concelebrants are holding the consecrated bread in their hands, they consume it at this time.[51]

Receiving the Precious Blood

48. The Precious Blood is received[52] in one of the following ways: The concelebrants approach the altar one after another or, if two chalices are used, two by two. They genuflect, partake of the Blood of Christ, wipe the rim of the chalice, and return to their seats, or the concelebrants may receive the Precious Blood while remaining in their places. They drink from the chalice presented to them by the deacon or one of the concelebrants, or else passed from one to the other. The chalice is wiped either by the one who drinks from it or by the one who presents it. The chalice is offered to each concelebrant without saying the formula *The Blood of Christ.*[53]

Alternate Form of Receiving Holy Communion

49. A second form of distributing Holy Communion to concelebrants is described by the *General Instruction.* "After the principal celebrant's Communion, the chalice is placed at the side of the altar on another corporal. The concelebrants approach the middle of the altar one by one, genuflect, and communicate from the Body of the Lord; then they move to the side of the altar and partake of the Blood of the Lord, following the rite chosen for Communion from the chalice, as has been remarked above."[54]

Communion by Intinction

50. "If the concelebrants' Communion is by intinction, the principal celebrant partakes of the Body and Blood of the Lord in the usual way, but making sure that enough of the precious Blood remains in the chalice for the Communion of the concelebrants. Then the Deacon, or one of the concelebrants, arranges the chalice together with the paten containing particles of the host, if appropriate, either in the center of the altar or at

---

[51] See GIRM, no. 244.

[52] The following is excerpted from a circular letter to the Presidents of Episcopal Conferences from Cardinal Joseph Ratzinger, Prefect of the Congregation for the Doctrine of the Faith (Prot. 89/78): "Concerning permission to use *mustum*: (A) The preferred solution continues to be Communion *per intinctionem*, or in concelebration under the species of bread alone. . . . (D) In general, those who have received permission to use *mustum* are prohibited from presiding at concelebrated Masses. There may be some exceptions however: in the case of a Bishop or Superior General; or, with prior approval of the Ordinary, at the celebration of the anniversary of priestly ordination or other similar occasions. In these cases, the one who presides is to communicate under both the species of bread and that of *mustum*, while for the other concelebrants a chalice shall be provided in which normal wine is to be consecrated."

[53] See GIRM, no. 246.

[54] GIRM, no. 248.

the side on another corporal. The concelebrants approach the altar one by one, genuflect, and take a particle, intinct it partly into the chalice, and, holding a purificator under their mouth, consume the intincted particle. They then return to their places as at the beginning of Mass."[55]

Distribution of Holy Communion to the Faithful

51. If there are many concelebrating priests, the Communion of the liturgical assembly should not be delayed. There is no need for all the concelebrants to finish receiving Holy Communion before distribution to the assembly can commence.

Purification of Sacred Vessels

52. After Communion, the Precious Blood is to be consumed immediately.[56] The sacred vessels are purified or are covered on a side table to be purified after Mass.[57]

Reverence to the Altar

53. Before leaving it, the concelebrants make a profound bow to the altar when the principal celebrant with the deacon venerates the altar with a kiss.[58] If the tabernacle is present in the sanctuary, they genuflect to it.

[55] GIRM, no. 249.
[56] See GIRM, no. 182.
[57] See GIRM, no. 183.
[58] See GIRM, no. 251.

EUCHARISTIC PRAYERS

I

II

III

IV

INRI

EUCHARISTIC PRAYER I

(THE ROMAN CANON)

for Concelebration

The parts for all concelebrants are to be recited in a low voice and in such a way that the voice of the principal celebrant is clearly heard by the people. (See GIRM, 218.)

84. The principal celebrant, with hands extended, says:

To you, therefore, most merciful Father,
we make humble prayer and petition
through Jesus Christ, your Son, our Lord:

He joins his hands and says:

that you accept

He makes the Sign of the Cross once over the bread and chalice together, saying:

and bless ✠ these gifts, these offerings,
these holy and unblemished sacrifices,

With hands extended, he continues:

which we offer you firstly
for your holy catholic Church.
Be pleased to grant her peace,
to guard, unite and govern her
throughout the whole world,
together with your servant N. **our Pope**
and N. **our Bishop,***
and all those who, holding to the truth,
hand on the catholic and apostolic faith.

He joins his hands.

85. **COMMEMORATION OF THE LIVING.**

With hands extended, one of the concelebrants or the principal celebrant, continues:

Remember, Lord, your servants N. **and** N.

The Priest joins his hands and all pray briefly for those for whom they intend to pray.

* Mention may be made here of the Coadjutor Bishop, or Auxiliary Bishops, as noted in the *General Instruction of the Roman Missal*, no. 149.

Then, with hands extended, he continues:

and all gathered here,
whose faith and devotion are known to you.
For them, we offer you this sacrifice of praise
or they offer it for themselves
and all who are dear to them:
for the redemption of their souls,
in hope of health and well-being,
and paying their homage to you,
the eternal God, living and true.

He joins his hands.

86. With hands extended, another of the concelebrants or the principal celebrant, continues:

In communion with those whose memory we venerate,
especially the glorious ever-Virgin Mary,
Mother of our God and Lord, Jesus Christ,
† and blessed Joseph, her Spouse,
your blessed Apostles and Martyrs,
Peter and Paul, Andrew,
(James, John,
Thomas, James, Philip,
Bartholomew, Matthew,
Simon and Jude;
Linus, Cletus, Clement, Sixtus,
Cornelius, Cyprian,
Lawrence, Chrysogonus,
John and Paul,
Cosmas and Damian)
and all your Saints;
we ask that through their merits and prayers,
in all things we may be defended
by your protecting help.

He joins he hands.

(Through Christ our Lord. Amen.)

PROPER FORMS OF THE *COMMUNICANTES*

On the Nativity of the Lord and throughout the Octave

Celebrating the most sacred night (day)
on which blessed Mary the immaculate Virgin
brought forth the Savior for this world,
and in communion with those whose memory we venerate,
especially the glorious ever-Virgin Mary,
Mother of our God and Lord, Jesus Christ, †

On the Epiphany of the Lord

Celebrating the most sacred day
on which your Only Begotten Son,
eternal with you in your glory,
appeared in a human body, truly sharing our flesh,
and in communion with those whose memory we venerate,
especially the glorious ever-Virgin Mary,
Mother of our God and Lord, Jesus Christ, †

From the Mass of the Easter Vigil until the Second Sunday of Easter

Celebrating the most sacred night (day)
of the Resurrection of our Lord Jesus Christ in the flesh,
and in communion with those whose memory we venerate,
especially the glorious ever-Virgin Mary,
Mother of our God and Lord, Jesus Christ, †

On the Ascension of the Lord

Celebrating the most sacred day
on which your Only Begotten Son, our Lord,
placed at the right hand of your glory
our weak human nature,
which he had united to himself,
and in communion with those whose memory we venerate,
especially the glorious ever-Virgin Mary,
Mother of our God and Lord, Jesus Christ, †

On Pentecost Sunday

Celebrating the most sacred day of Pentecost,
on which the Holy Spirit
appeared to the Apostles in tongues of fire,
and in communion with those whose memory we venerate,
especially the glorious ever-Virgin Mary,
Mother of our God and Lord, Jesus Christ, †

87. With hands extended, the principal celebrant alone continues:

Therefore, Lord, we pray:
graciously accept this oblation of our service,
that of your whole family;
order our days in your peace,
and command that we be delivered from eternal damnation
and counted among the flock of those you have chosen.

He joins his hands.

(Through Christ our Lord. Amen.)

88. The principal celebrant and all concelebrants, holding their hands extended toward the offerings, say:

Be pleased, O God, we pray,
to bless, acknowledge,
and approve this offering in every respect;
make it spiritual and acceptable,
so that it may become for us
the Body and Blood of your most beloved Son,
our Lord Jesus Christ.

89. They join their hands.

On the day before he was to suffer,
he took bread in his holy and venerable hands,
and with eyes raised to heaven
to you, O God, his almighty Father,
giving you thanks, he said the blessing,
broke the bread
and gave it to his disciples, saying:

Each concelebrant extends his right hand toward the bread, if this seems appropriate.

TAKE THIS, ALL OF YOU, AND EAT OF IT,
FOR THIS IS MY BODY,
WHICH WILL BE GIVEN UP FOR YOU.

The concelebrants join their hands, look toward the consecrated host as it is shown, and after this bow profoundly.

90. Then all continue:

In a similar way, when supper was ended,
he took this precious chalice
in his holy and venerable hands,
and once more giving you thanks, he said the blessing
and gave the chalice to his disciples, saying:

Each concelebrant extends his right hand toward the chalice, if this seems appropriate.

TAKE THIS, ALL OF YOU, AND DRINK FROM IT,
FOR THIS IS THE CHALICE OF MY BLOOD,
THE BLOOD OF THE NEW AND ETERNAL COVENANT,
WHICH WILL BE POURED OUT FOR YOU AND FOR MANY
FOR THE FORGIVENESS OF SINS.

DO THIS IN MEMORY OF ME.

The concelebrants join their hands, look toward the chalice as it is shown, and after this bow profoundly.

91. Then the principal celebrant says:

The mystery of faith.

And the concelebrants with the people continue, acclaiming:

We proclaim your Death, O Lord,
and profess your Resurrection
until you come again.

Or:

When we eat this Bread and drink this Cup,
we proclaim your Death, O Lord,
until you come again.

Or:

Save us, Savior of the world,
for by your Cross and Resurrection
you have set us free.

92. Then the principal celebrant and the concelebrants, with hands extended, say:

**Therefore, O Lord,
as we celebrate the memorial of the blessed Passion,
the Resurrection from the dead,
and the glorious Ascension into heaven
of Christ, your Son, our Lord,
we, your servants and your holy people,
offer to your glorious majesty
from the gifts that you have given us,
this pure victim,
this holy victim,
this spotless victim,
the holy Bread of eternal life
and the Chalice of everlasting salvation.**

93. **Be pleased to look upon these offerings
with a serene and kindly countenance,
and to accept them,
as once you were pleased to accept
the gifts of your servant Abel the just,
the sacrifice of Abraham, our father in faith,
and the offering of your high priest Melchizedek,
a holy sacrifice, a spotless victim.**

94. Bowing, with hands joined, all continue:

**In humble prayer we ask you, almighty God:
command that these gifts be borne
by the hands of your holy Angel
to your altar on high
in the sight of your divine majesty,
so that all of us, who through this participation at the altar
receive the most holy Body and Blood of your Son,**

They stand upright again and sign themselves with the Sign of the Cross, saying:

may be filled with every grace and heavenly blessing.

They join their hands.

(Through Christ our Lord. Amen.)

95. **COMMEMORATION OF THE DEAD.**

With hands extended, one of the concelebrants or the principal celebrant says:

**Remember also, Lord, your servants N. and N.,
who have gone before us with the sign of faith
and rest in the sleep of peace.**

He joins his hands, and all pray briefly for those who have died and for whom they intend to pray.

Then, with hands extended, he continues:

**Grant them, O Lord, we pray,
and all who sleep in Christ,
a place of refreshment, light and peace.**

He joins his hands.

(Through Christ our Lord. Amen.)

96. All strike their breast with the right hand as another of the concelebrants or the principal celebrant says:

To us, also, your servants, who, though sinners,

And, with hands extended, he continues:

**hope in your abundant mercies,
graciously grant some share
and fellowship with your holy Apostles and Martyrs:
with John the Baptist, Stephen,
Matthias, Barnabas,
(Ignatius, Alexander,
Marcellinus, Peter,
Felicity, Perpetua,
Agatha, Lucy,
Agnes, Cecilia, Anastasia)
and all your Saints;
admit us, we beseech you,
into their company,
not weighing our merits,
but granting us your pardon,**

He joins his hands.

through Christ our Lord.

97. And the principal celebrant alone, with hands joined, continues:

Through whom
you continue to make all these good things, O Lord;
you sanctify them, fill them with life,
bless them, and bestow them upon us.

98. The principal celebrant raises the paten with the host, and the deacon, or in his absence, one of the concelebrants, raises the chalice, while the principal celebrant alone, or with all the concelebrants, says:

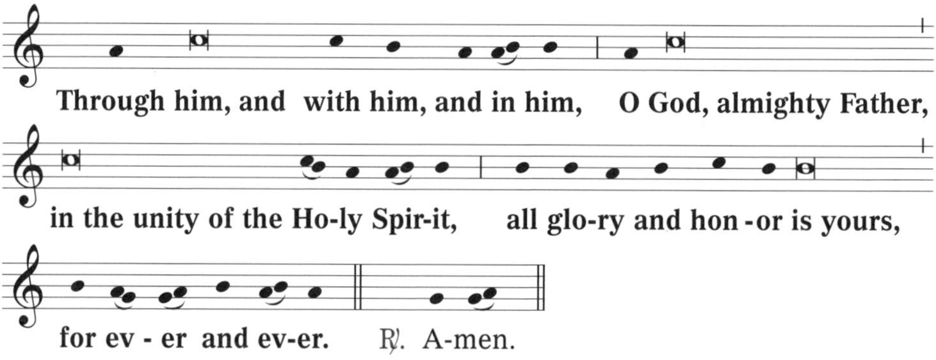
Through him, and with him, and in him, O God, almighty Father,
in the unity of the Ho-ly Spir-it, all glo-ry and hon -or is yours,
for ev - er and ev-er. ℟. A-men.

Through him, and with him, and in him,
O God, almighty Father,
in the unity of the Holy Spirit,
all glory and honor is yours,
for ever and ever.

The people acclaim:

Amen.

EUCHARISTIC PRAYER II

for Concelebration

The parts for all concelebrants are to be recited in a low voice and in such a way that the voice of the principal celebrant is clearly heard by the people. (See GIRM, 218.)

100. The principal celebrant, with hands extended, says:

You are indeed Holy, O Lord,
the fount of all holiness.

101. The principal celebrant and all concelebrants, holding their hands extended toward the offerings, say:

Make holy, therefore, these gifts, we pray,
by sending down your Spirit upon them
like the dewfall,

The principal celebrant joins his hands and makes the Sign of the Cross once over the bread and the chalice together, saying:

so that they may become for us
the Body and ✠ Blood of our Lord Jesus Christ.

102. They join their hands.

At the time he was betrayed
and entered willingly into his Passion,
he took bread and, giving thanks, broke it,
and gave it to his disciples, saying:

Each concelebrant extends his right hand toward the bread, if this seems appropriate.

TAKE THIS, ALL OF YOU, AND EAT OF IT,
FOR THIS IS MY BODY,
WHICH WILL BE GIVEN UP FOR YOU.

The concelebrants join their hands, look toward the consecrated host as it is shown, and after this bow profoundly.

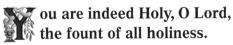

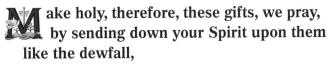

103. After this, the principal celebrant and all concelebrants continue:

In a similar way, when supper was ended,
he took the chalice
and, once more giving thanks,
he gave it to his disciples, saying:

Each concelebrant extends his right hand toward the chalice, if this seems appropriate.

TAKE THIS, ALL OF YOU, AND DRINK FROM IT,
FOR THIS IS THE CHALICE OF MY BLOOD,
THE BLOOD OF THE NEW AND ETERNAL COVENANT,
WHICH WILL BE POURED OUT FOR YOU AND FOR MANY
FOR THE FORGIVENESS OF SINS.

DO THIS IN MEMORY OF ME.

The concelebrants join their hands, look toward the chalice as it is shown, and after this bow profoundly.

104. Then the principal celebrant says:

The mystery of faith.

And the concelebrants with the people continue, acclaiming:

We proclaim your Death, O Lord,
and profess your Resurrection
until you come again.

Or:

When we eat this Bread and drink this Cup,
we proclaim your Death, O Lord,
until you come again.

Or:

Save us, Savior of the world,
for by your Cross and Resurrection
you have set us free.

105. Then the principal celebrant and the concelebrants, with hands extended, say:

Therefore, as we celebrate
the memorial of his Death and Resurrection,
we offer you, Lord,
the Bread of life and the Chalice of salvation,
giving thanks that you have held us worthy
to be in your presence and minister to you.

Humbly we pray
that, partaking of the Body and Blood of Christ,
we may be gathered into one by the Holy Spirit.

They join their hands.

With hands extended, one of the concelebrants or the principal celebrant says:

Remember, Lord, your Church,
spread throughout the world,
and bring her to the fullness of charity,
together with N. **our Pope and** N. **our Bishop***
and all the clergy.

He joins his hands.

* Mention may be made here of the Coadjutor Bishop, or Auxiliary Bishops, as noted in the *General Instruction of the Roman Missal*, no. 149.

With hands extended, another of the concelebrants or the principal celebrant says:

In Masses for the Dead, the following may be added:

Remember your servant N.,
whom you have called (today)
from this world to yourself.
Grant that he (she) who was united with your Son
in a death like his,
may also be one with him in his Resurrection.

Remember also our brothers and sisters
who have fallen asleep in the hope of the resurrection,
and all who have died in your mercy:
welcome them into the light of your face.
Have mercy on us all, we pray,
that with the Blessed Virgin Mary, Mother of God,
with the blessed Apostles,
and all the Saints who have pleased you throughout the ages,
we may merit to be coheirs to eternal life,
and may praise and glorify you

He joins his hands.

through your Son, Jesus Christ.

106. The principal celebrant raises the paten with the host, and the deacon, or in his absence, one of the concelebrants, raises the chalice, while the principal celebrant alone, or with all the concelebrants, says:

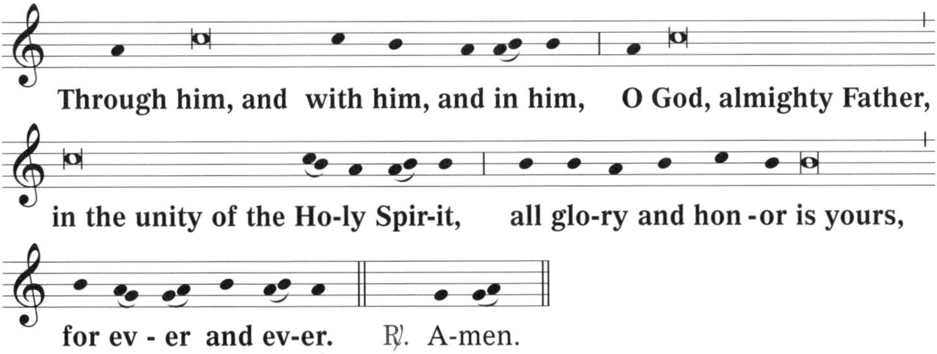
Through him, and with him, and in him, O God, almighty Father,
in the unity of the Ho-ly Spir-it, all glo-ry and hon-or is yours,
for ev - er and ev-er. R/. A-men.

Through him, and with him, and in him,
O God, almighty Father,
in the unity of the Holy Spirit,
all glory and honor is yours,
for ever and ever.

The people acclaim:

Amen.

EUCHARISTIC PRAYER III

for Concelebration

The parts for all concelebrants are to be recited in a low voice and in such a way that the voice of the principal celebrant is clearly heard by the people. (See GIRM, 218.)

108. The principal celebrant, with hands extended, says:

You are indeed Holy, O Lord,
and all you have created
rightly gives you praise,
for through your Son our Lord Jesus Christ,
by the power and working of the Holy Spirit,
you give life to all things and make them holy,
and you never cease to gather a people to yourself,
so that from the rising of the sun to its setting
a pure sacrifice may be offered to your name.

109. The principal celebrant and all concelebrants, holding their hands extended toward the offerings, say:

Therefore, O Lord, we humbly implore you:
by the same Spirit graciously make holy
these gifts we have brought to you for consecration,

The principal celebrant joins his hands and makes the Sign of the Cross once over the bread and chalice together, saying:

that they may become the Body and ✠ Blood
of your Son our Lord Jesus Christ,

They join their hands.

at whose command we celebrate these mysteries.

110.

For on the night he was betrayed
he himself took bread,
and, giving you thanks, he said the blessing,
broke the bread and gave it to his disciples, saying:

Each concelebrant extends his right hand toward the bread, if this seems appropriate.

TAKE THIS, ALL OF YOU, AND EAT OF IT,
FOR THIS IS MY BODY,
WHICH WILL BE GIVEN UP FOR YOU.

The concelebrants join their hands, look toward the consecrated host as it is shown, and after this bow profoundly.

111. After this, the principal celebrant and all concelebrants continue:

In a similar way, when supper was ended,
he took the chalice,
and, giving you thanks, he said the blessing,
and gave the chalice to his disciples, saying:

Each concelebrant extends his right hand toward the chalice, if this seems appropriate.

TAKE THIS, ALL OF YOU, AND DRINK FROM IT,
FOR THIS IS THE CHALICE OF MY BLOOD,
THE BLOOD OF THE NEW AND ETERNAL COVENANT,
WHICH WILL BE POURED OUT FOR YOU AND FOR MANY
FOR THE FORGIVENESS OF SINS.

DO THIS IN MEMORY OF ME.

The concelebrants join their hands, look toward the chalice as it is shown, and after this bow profoundly.

112. Then the principal celebrant says:

The mystery of faith.

And the concelebrants with the people continue, acclaiming:

We proclaim your Death, O Lord,
and profess your Resurrection
until you come again.

Or:

When we eat this Bread and drink this Cup,
we proclaim your Death, O Lord,
until you come again.

Or:

Save us, Savior of the world,
for by your Cross and Resurrection
you have set us free.

113. Then the principal celebrant and the concelebrants, with hands extended, say:

Therefore, O Lord, as we celebrate the memorial
of the saving Passion of your Son,
his wondrous Resurrection
and Ascension into heaven,
and as we look forward to his second coming,
we offer you in thanksgiving
this holy and living sacrifice.

Look, we pray, upon the oblation of your Church
and, recognizing the sacrificial Victim by whose death
you willed to reconcile us to yourself,
grant that we, who are nourished
by the Body and Blood of your Son
and filled with his Holy Spirit,
may become one body, one spirit in Christ.

They join their hands.

With hands extended, one of the concelebrants or the principal celebrant says:

May he make of us
an eternal offering to you,
so that we may obtain an inheritance with your elect,
especially with the most Blessed Virgin Mary, Mother of God,
with your blessed Apostles and glorious Martyrs
(with Saint N.: the Saint of the day or Patron Saint**)**
and with all the Saints,
on whose constant intercession in your presence
we rely for unfailing help.

He joins his hands.

With hands extended, another of the concelebrants or the principal celebrant says:

May this Sacrifice of our reconciliation,
we pray, O Lord,
advance the peace and salvation of all the world.
Be pleased to confirm in faith and charity
your pilgrim Church on earth,
with your servant N. our Pope and N. our Bishop,*
the Order of Bishops, all the clergy,
and the entire people you have gained for your own.

* Mention may be made here of the Coadjutor Bishop, or Auxiliary Bishops, as noted in the *General Instruction of the Roman Missal*, no. 149.

Listen graciously to the prayers of this family,
whom you have summoned before you:
in your compassion, O merciful Father,
gather to yourself all your children
scattered throughout the world.

He joins his hands.

With hands extended, another of the concelebrants or the principal celebrant says:

† **To our departed brothers and sisters**
and to all who were pleasing to you
at their passing from this life,
give kind admittance to your kingdom.
There we hope to enjoy for ever the fullness of your glory

He joins his hands.

through Christ our Lord,
through whom you bestow on the world all that is good. †

114. The principal celebrant raises the paten with the host, and the deacon, or in his absence, one of the concelebrants, raises the chalice, while the principal celebrant alone, or with all the concelebrants, says:

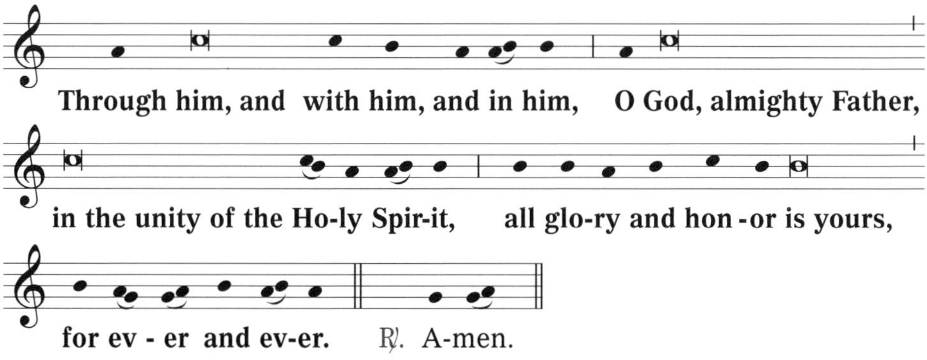
Through him, and with him, and in him, O God, almighty Father,
in the unity of the Ho-ly Spir-it, all glo-ry and hon -or is yours,
for ev - er and ev-er. ℟. A-men.

Through him, and with him, and in him,
O God, almighty Father,
in the unity of the Holy Spirit,
all glory and honor is yours,
for ever and ever.

The people acclaim:

Amen.

115. When this Eucharistic Prayer is used in Masses for the Dead, the following may be said:

† Remember your servant N.
whom you have called (today)
from this world to yourself.
Grant that he (she) who was united with your Son
in a death like his,
may also be one with him in his Resurrection,
when from the earth
he will raise up in the flesh those who have died,
and transform our lowly body
after the pattern of his own glorious body.
To our departed brothers and sisters, too,
and to all who were pleasing to you
at their passing from this life,
give kind admittance to your kingdom.
There we hope to enjoy for ever the fullness of your glory,
when you will wipe away every tear from our eyes.
For seeing you, our God, as you are,
we shall be like you for all the ages
and praise you without end,

He joins his hands.

through Christ our Lord,
through whom you bestow on the world all that is good. †

EUCHARISTIC PRAYER IV

for Concelebration

The parts for all concelebrants are to be recited in a low voice and in such a way that the voice of the principal celebrant is clearly heard by the people. (See GIRM, 218.)

117. The principal celebrant, with hands extended, says:

We give you praise, Father most holy,
for you are great
and you have fashioned all your works
in wisdom and in love.
You formed man in your own image
and entrusted the whole world to his care,
so that in serving you alone, the Creator,
he might have dominion over all creatures.
And when through disobedience he had lost your friendship,
you did not abandon him to the domain of death.
For you came in mercy to the aid of all,
so that those who seek might find you.
Time and again you offered them covenants
and through the prophets
taught them to look forward to salvation.

And you so loved the world, Father most holy,
that in the fullness of time
you sent your Only Begotten Son to be our Savior.
Made incarnate by the Holy Spirit
and born of the Virgin Mary,
he shared our human nature
in all things but sin.
To the poor he proclaimed the good news of salvation,
to prisoners, freedom,
and to the sorrowful of heart, joy.
To accomplish your plan,
he gave himself up to death,
and, rising from the dead,
he destroyed death and restored life.

And that we might live no longer for ourselves
but for him who died and rose again for us,
he sent the Holy Spirit from you, Father,
as the first fruits for those who believe,
so that, bringing to perfection his work in the world,
he might sanctify creation to the full.

118. The principal celebrant and all concelebrants, holding their hands extended toward the offerings, say:

Therefore, O Lord, we pray:
may this same Holy Spirit
graciously sanctify these offerings,

The principal celebrant joins his hands and makes the Sign of the Cross once over the bread and chalice together, saying:

that they may become
the Body and ✠ Blood of our Lord Jesus Christ

They join their hands.

for the celebration of this great mystery,
which he himself left us
as an eternal covenant.

119.

For when the hour had come
for him to be glorified by you, Father most holy,
having loved his own who were in the world,
he loved them to the end:
and while they were at supper,
he took bread, blessed and broke it,
and gave it to his disciples, saying:

Each concelebrant extends his right hand toward the bread, if this seems appropriate.

TAKE THIS, ALL OF YOU, AND EAT OF IT,
FOR THIS IS MY BODY,
WHICH WILL BE GIVEN UP FOR YOU.

The concelebrants join their hands, look toward the consecrated host as it is shown, and after this bow profoundly.

120. After this, the principal celebrant and all concelebrants continue:

In a similar way,
taking the chalice filled with the fruit of the vine,
he gave thanks,
and gave the chalice to his disciples, saying:

Each concelebrant extends his right hand toward the chalice, if this seems appropriate.

TAKE THIS, ALL OF YOU, AND DRINK FROM IT,
FOR THIS IS THE CHALICE OF MY BLOOD,
THE BLOOD OF THE NEW AND ETERNAL COVENANT,
WHICH WILL BE POURED OUT FOR YOU AND FOR MANY
FOR THE FORGIVENESS OF SINS.

DO THIS IN MEMORY OF ME.

The concelebrants join their hands, look toward the chalice as it is shown, and after this bow profoundly.

121. Then the principal celebrant says:

The mystery of faith.

And the concelebrants with the people continue, acclaiming:

We proclaim your Death, O Lord,
and profess your Resurrection
until you come again.

Or:

When we eat this Bread and drink this Cup,
we proclaim your Death, O Lord,
until you come again.

Or:

Save us, Savior of the world,
for by your Cross and Resurrection
you have set us free.

122. Then the principal celebrant and the concelebrants, with hands extended, say:

Therefore, O Lord,
as we now celebrate the memorial of our redemption,
we remember Christ's Death
and his descent to the realm of the dead,
we proclaim his Resurrection
and his Ascension to your right hand,
and, as we await his coming in glory,
we offer you his Body and Blood,
the sacrifice acceptable to you
which brings salvation to the whole world.

Look, O Lord, upon the Sacrifice
which you yourself have provided for your Church,
and grant in your loving kindness
to all who partake of this one Bread and one Chalice
that, gathered into one body by the Holy Spirit,
they may truly become a living sacrifice in Christ
to the praise of your glory.

They join their hands.

With hands extended, one of the concelebrants or the principal celebrant says:

Therefore, Lord, remember now
all for whom we offer this sacrifice:
especially your servant N. our Pope,
N. our Bishop,* and the whole Order of Bishops,
all the clergy,
those who take part in this offering,
those gathered here before you,
your entire people,
and all who seek you with a sincere heart.

Remember also
those who have died in the peace of your Christ
and all the dead,
whose faith you alone have known.

He joins his hands.

---

* Mention may be made here of the Coadjutor Bishop, or Auxiliary Bishops, as noted in the *General Instruction of the Roman Missal*, no. 149.

With hands extended, another of the concelebrants or the principal celebrant says:

To all of us, your children,
grant, O merciful Father,
that we may enter into a heavenly inheritance
with the Blessed Virgin Mary, Mother of God,
and with your Apostles and Saints in your kingdom.
There, with the whole of creation,
freed from the corruption of sin and death,
may we glorify you through Christ our Lord,

He joins his hands.

through whom you bestow on the world all that is good.

123. The principal celebrant raises the paten with the host, and the deacon, or in his absence, one of the concelebrants, raises the chalice, while the principal celebrant alone, or with all the concelebrants, says:

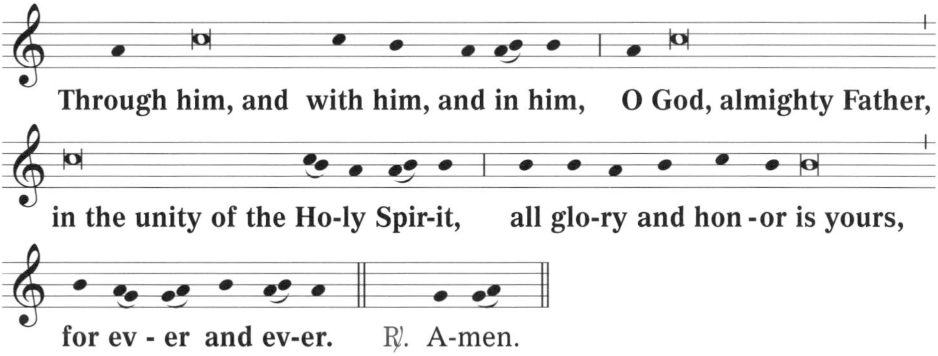
Through him, and with him, and in him, O God, almighty Father,
in the unity of the Ho-ly Spir-it, all glo-ry and hon -or is yours,
for ev - er and ev-er. ℟. A-men.

Through him, and with him, and in him,
O God, almighty Father,
in the unity of the Holy Spirit,
all glory and honor is yours,
for ever and ever.

The people acclaim:

Amen.

EUCHARISTIC PRAYERS FOR RECONCILIATION

R 1

R 2

EUCHARISTIC PRAYERS FOR USE IN MASSES FOR VARIOUS NEEDS

V 1

V 2

V 3

V 4

EUCHARISTIC PRAYER FOR RECONCILIATION I

for Concelebration

The parts for all concelebrants are to be recited in a low voice and in such a way that the voice of the principal celebrant is clearly heard by the people. (See GIRM, 218.)

2. The principal celebrant, with hands extended, says:

You are indeed Holy, O Lord,
and from the world's beginning
are ceaselessly at work,
so that the human race may become holy,
just as you yourself are holy.

3. The principal celebrant and all concelebrants, holding their hands extended toward the offerings, say:

Look, we pray, upon your people's offerings
and pour out on them the power of your Spirit,

The principal celebrant joins his hands and makes the Sign of the Cross once over the bread and chalice together, saying:

that they may become the Body and ✠ Blood

They join their hands.

of your beloved Son, Jesus Christ,
in whom we, too, are your sons and daughters.

Indeed, though we once were lost
and could not approach you,
you loved us with the greatest love:
for your Son, who alone is just,
handed himself over to death,
and did not disdain to be nailed for our sake
to the wood of the Cross.

But before his arms were outstretched between heaven and earth,
to become the lasting sign of your covenant,
he desired to celebrate the Passover with his disciples.

4. **As he ate with them,**
he took bread
and, giving you thanks, he said the blessing,
broke the bread and gave it to them, saying:

Each concelebrant extends his right hand toward the bread, if this seems appropriate.

TAKE THIS, ALL OF YOU, AND EAT OF IT,

FOR THIS IS MY BODY,

WHICH WILL BE GIVEN UP FOR YOU.

The concelebrants join their hands, look toward the consecrated host as it is shown, and after this bow profoundly.

5. After this, the principal celebrant and all concelebrants continue:

In a similar way, when supper was ended,
knowing that he was about to reconcile all things in himself
through his Blood to be shed on the Cross,
he took the chalice, filled with the fruit of the vine,
and once more giving you thanks,
handed the chalice to his disciples, saying:

Each concelebrant extends his right hand toward the chalice, if this seems appropriate.

TAKE THIS, ALL OF YOU, AND DRINK FROM IT,

FOR THIS IS THE CHALICE OF MY BLOOD,

THE BLOOD OF THE NEW AND ETERNAL COVENANT,

WHICH WILL BE POURED OUT FOR YOU AND FOR MANY

FOR THE FORGIVENESS OF SINS.

DO THIS IN MEMORY OF ME.

The concelebrants join their hands, look toward the chalice as it is shown, and after this bow profoundly.

6. Then the principal celebrant says:

The mystery of faith.

And the concelebrants with the people continue, acclaiming:

We proclaim your Death, O Lord,
and profess your Resurrection
until you come again.

Or:

When we eat this Bread and drink this Cup,
we proclaim your Death, O Lord,
until you come again.

Or:

Save us, Savior of the world,
for by your Cross and Resurrection
you have set us free.

7. Then the principal celebrant and the concelebrants, with hands extended, say:

**Therefore, as we celebrate
the memorial of your Son Jesus Christ,
who is our Passover and our surest peace,
we celebrate his Death and Resurrection from the dead,
and looking forward to his blessed Coming,
we offer you, who are our faithful and merciful God,
this sacrificial Victim
who reconciles to you the human race.**

**Look kindly, most compassionate Father,
on those you unite to yourself
by the Sacrifice of your Son,
and grant that, by the power of the Holy Spirit,
as they partake of this one Bread and one Chalice,
they may be gathered into one Body in Christ,
who heals every division.**

They join their hands.

With hands extended, one of the concelebrants or the principal celebrant says:

Be pleased to keep us always
in communion of mind and heart,
together with N. our Pope and N. our Bishop. *
Help us to work together
for the coming of your Kingdom,
until the hour when we stand before you,
Saints among the Saints in the halls of heaven,
with the Blessed Virgin Mary, Mother of God,
the blessed Apostles and all the Saints,
and with our deceased brothers and sisters,
whom we humbly commend to your mercy.

Then, freed at last from the wound of corruption
and made fully into a new creation,
we shall sing to you with gladness

He joins his hands.

the thanksgiving of Christ,
who lives for all eternity.

---

* Mention may be made here of the Coadjutor Bishop, or Auxiliary Bishops, as noted in the *General Instruction of the Roman Missal*, no. 149.

8. The principal celebrant raises the paten with the host, and the deacon, or in his absence, one of the concelebrants, raises the chalice, while the principal celebrant alone, or with all the concelebrants, says:

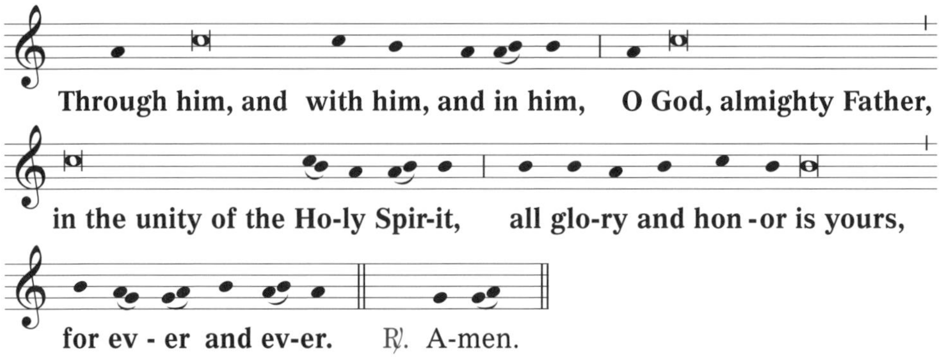
Through him, and with him, and in him, O God, almighty Father,
in the unity of the Ho-ly Spir-it, all glo-ry and hon -or is yours,
for ev - er and ev-er. ℟. A-men.

Through him, and with him, and in him,
O God, almighty Father,
in the unity of the Holy Spirit,
all glory and honor is yours,
for ever and ever.

The people acclaim:

Amen.

EUCHARISTIC PRAYER FOR RECONCILIATION II

for Concelebration

The parts for all concelebrants are to be recited in a low voice and in such a way that the voice of the principal celebrant is clearly heard by the people. (See GIRM, 218.)

2. The principal celebrant, with hands extended, says:

You, therefore, almighty Father,
we bless through Jesus Christ your Son,
who comes in your name.
He himself is the Word that brings salvation,
the hand you extend to sinners,
the way by which your peace is offered to us.
When we ourselves had turned away from you
on account of our sins,
you brought us back to be reconciled, O Lord,
so that, converted at last to you,
we might love one another
through your Son,
whom for our sake you handed over to death.

3. The principal celebrant and all concelebrants, holding their hands extended toward the offerings, say:

And now, celebrating the reconciliation
Christ has brought us,
we entreat you:
sanctify these gifts by the outpouring of your Spirit,

The principal celebrant joins his hands and makes the Sign of the Cross once over the bread and chalice together, saying:

that they may become the Body and ✠ Blood of your Son,
whose command we fulfill
when we celebrate these mysteries.

4. They join their hands.

For when about to give his life to set us free,
as he reclined at supper,
he himself took bread into his hands,
and, giving you thanks, he said the blessing,
broke the bread and gave it to his disciples, saying:

Each concelebrant extends his right hand toward the bread, if this seems appropriate.

TAKE THIS, ALL OF YOU, AND EAT OF IT,
FOR THIS IS MY BODY,
WHICH WILL BE GIVEN UP FOR YOU.

The concelebrants join their hands, look toward the consecrated host as it is shown, and after this bow profoundly.

5. After this, the principal celebrant and all concelebrants continue:

In a similar way, on that same evening,
he took the chalice of blessing in his hands,
confessing your mercy,
and gave the chalice to his disciples, saying:

Each concelebrant extends his right hand toward the chalice, if this seems appropriate.

TAKE THIS, ALL OF YOU, AND DRINK FROM IT,
FOR THIS IS THE CHALICE OF MY BLOOD,
THE BLOOD OF THE NEW AND ETERNAL COVENANT,
WHICH WILL BE POURED OUT FOR YOU AND FOR MANY
FOR THE FORGIVENESS OF SINS.

DO THIS IN MEMORY OF ME.

The concelebrants join their hands, look toward the chalice as it is shown, and after this bow profoundly.

6. Then the principal celebrant says:

The mystery of faith.

And the concelebrants with the people continue, acclaiming:

We proclaim your Death, O Lord,
and profess your Resurrection
until you come again.

Or:

When we eat this Bread and drink this Cup,
we proclaim your Death, O Lord,
until you come again.

Or:

Save us, Savior of the world,
for by your Cross and Resurrection
you have set us free.

7. Then the principal celebrant and the concelebrants, with hands extended, say:

Celebrating, therefore, the memorial
of the Death and Resurrection of your Son,
who left us this pledge of his love,
we offer you what you have bestowed on us,
the Sacrifice of perfect reconciliation.

Holy Father, we humbly beseech you
to accept us also, together with your Son,
and in this saving banquet
graciously to endow us with his very Spirit,
who takes away everything
that estranges us from one another.

They join their hands.

With hands extended, one of the concelebrants or the principal celebrant says:

May he make your Church a sign of unity
and an instrument of your peace among all people
and may he keep us in communion
with N. **our Pope and** N. **our Bishop** *
and all the Bishops
and your entire people.

He joins his hands.

---

* Mention may be made here of the Coadjutor Bishop, or Auxiliary Bishops, as noted in the *General Instruction of the Roman Missal*, no. 149.

With hands extended, another of the concelebrants or the principal celebrant says:

Just as you have gathered us now at the table of your Son,
so also bring us together,
with the glorious Virgin Mary, Mother of God,
with your blessed Apostles and all the Saints,
with our brothers and sisters
and those of every race and tongue
who have died in your friendship.
Bring us to share with them the unending banquet of unity
in a new heaven and a new earth,
where the fullness of your peace will shine forth

He joins his hands.

in Christ Jesus our Lord.

8. The principal celebrant raises the paten with the host, and the deacon, or in his absence, one of the concelebrants, raises the chalice, while the principal celebrant alone, or with all the concelebrants, says:

Through him, and with him, and in him, O God, almighty Father,
in the unity of the Ho-ly Spir-it, all glo-ry and hon -or is yours,
for ev - er and ev-er. ℟. A-men.

Through him, and with him, and in him,
O God, almighty Father,
in the unity of the Holy Spirit,
all glory and honor is yours,
for ever and ever.

The people acclaim:

Amen.

EUCHARISTIC PRAYER FOR USE IN MASSES FOR VARIOUS NEEDS I

The Church on the Path of Unity

for Concelebration

The parts for all concelebrants are to be recited in a low voice and in such a way that the voice of the principal celebrant is clearly heard by the people. (See GIRM, 218.)

2. The principal celebrant, with hands extended, says:

You are indeed Holy and to be glorified, O God,
who love the human race
and who always walk with us on the journey of life.
Blessed indeed is your Son,
present in our midst
when we are gathered by his love
and when, as once for the disciples, so now for us,
he opens the Scriptures and breaks the bread.

3. The principal celebrant and all concelebrants, holding their hands extended toward the offerings, say:

Therefore, Father most merciful,
we ask that you send forth your Holy Spirit
to sanctify these gifts of bread and wine,

The principal celebrant joins his hands and makes the Sign of the Cross once over the bread and chalice together, saying:

that they may become for us
the Body and ✠ Blood

They join their hands.

of our Lord Jesus Christ.

4.

On the day before he was to suffer,
on the night of the Last Supper,
he took bread and said the blessing,
broke the bread and gave it to his disciples, saying:

Each concelebrant extends his right hand toward the bread, if this seems appropriate.

TAKE THIS, ALL OF YOU, AND EAT OF IT,
FOR THIS IS MY BODY,
WHICH WILL BE GIVEN UP FOR YOU.

The concelebrants join their hands, look toward the consecrated host as it is shown, and after this bow profoundly.

5. After this, the principal celebrant and all concelebrants continue:

In a similar way, when supper was ended,
he took the chalice, gave you thanks
and gave the chalice to his disciples, saying:

Each concelebrant extends his right hand toward the chalice, if this seems appropriate.

TAKE THIS, ALL OF YOU, AND DRINK FROM IT,
FOR THIS IS THE CHALICE OF MY BLOOD,
THE BLOOD OF THE NEW AND ETERNAL COVENANT,
WHICH WILL BE POURED OUT FOR YOU AND FOR MANY
FOR THE FORGIVENESS OF SINS.

DO THIS IN MEMORY OF ME.

The concelebrants join their hands, look toward the chalice as it is shown, and after this bow profoundly.

6. Then the principal celebrant says:

The mystery of faith.

And the concelebrants with the people continue, acclaiming:

We proclaim your Death, O Lord,
and profess your Resurrection
until you come again.

Or:

When we eat this Bread and drink this Cup,
we proclaim your Death, O Lord,
until you come again.

Or:

Save us, Savior of the world,
for by your Cross and Resurrection
you have set us free.

7. Then the principal celebrant and the concelebrants, with hands extended, say:

Therefore, holy Father,
as we celebrate the memorial of Christ your Son,
our Savior,
whom you led through his Passion and Death on the Cross
to the glory of the Resurrection,
and whom you have seated at your right hand,
we proclaim the work of your love until he comes again
and we offer you the Bread of life
and the Chalice of blessing.

Look with favor on the oblation of your Church,
in which we show forth
the paschal Sacrifice of Christ that has been handed on to us,
and grant that, by the power of the Spirit of your love,
we may be counted now and until the day of eternity
among the members of your Son,
in whose Body and Blood we have communion.

They join their hands.

With hands extended, one of the concelebrants or the principal celebrant says:

Lord, renew your Church (which is in N.**)**
by the light of the Gospel.
Strengthen the bond of unity
between the faithful and the pastors of your people,
together with N. **our Pope,** N. **our Bishop,***
and the whole Order of Bishops,
that in a world torn by strife
your people may shine forth
as a prophetic sign of unity and concord.

He joins his hands.

---

* Mention may be made here of the Coadjutor Bishop, or Auxiliary Bishops, as noted in the *General Instruction of the Roman Missal*, no. 149.

With hands extended, another of the concelebrants or the principal celebrant says:

Remember our brothers and sisters (N. and N.),
who have fallen asleep in the peace of your Christ,
and all the dead, whose faith you alone have known.
Admit them to rejoice in the light of your face,
and in the resurrection give them the fullness of life.

Grant also to us,
when our earthly pilgrimage is done,
that we may come to an eternal dwelling place
and live with you for ever;
there, in communion with the Blessed Virgin Mary,
Mother of God,
with the Apostles and Martyrs,
(with Saint N.: the Saint of the day or Patron)
and with all the Saints,
we shall praise and exalt you

He joins his hands.

through Jesus Christ, your Son.

8. The principal celebrant raises the paten with the host, and the deacon, or in his absence, one of the concelebrants, raises the chalice, while the principal celebrant alone, or with all the concelebrants, says:

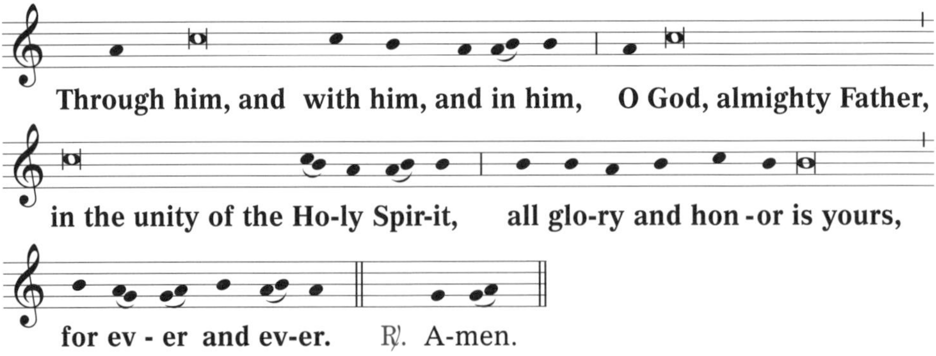
Through him, and with him, and in him, O God, almighty Father,
in the unity of the Ho-ly Spir-it, all glo-ry and hon -or is yours,
for ev - er and ev-er. ℟. A-men.

Through him, and with him, and in him,
O God, almighty Father,
in the unity of the Holy Spirit,
all glory and honor is yours,
for ever and ever.

The people acclaim:

Amen.

EUCHARISTIC PRAYER FOR USE IN MASSES FOR VARIOUS NEEDS II

God Guides His Church along the Way of Salvation

for Concelebration

The parts for all concelebrants are to be recited in a low voice and in such a way that the voice of the principal celebrant is clearly heard by the people. (See GIRM, 218.)

2. The principal celebrant, with hands extended, says:

**You are indeed Holy and to be glorified, O God,
who love the human race
and who always walk with us on the journey of life.
Blessed indeed is your Son,
present in our midst
when we are gathered by his love
and when, as once for the disciples, so now for us,
he opens the Scriptures and breaks the bread.**

3. The principal celebrant and all concelebrants, holding their hands extended toward the offerings, say:

**Therefore, Father most merciful,
we ask that you send forth your Holy Spirit
to sanctify these gifts of bread and wine,**

The principal celebrant joins his hands and makes the Sign of the Cross once over the bread and chalice together, saying:

**that they may become for us
the Body and ✠ Blood**

They join their hands.

of our Lord Jesus Christ.

4.

**On the day before he was to suffer,
on the night of the Last Supper,
he took bread and said the blessing,
broke the bread and gave it to his disciples, saying:**

Each concelebrant extends his right hand toward the bread, if this seems appropriate.

**TAKE THIS, ALL OF YOU, AND EAT OF IT,
FOR THIS IS MY BODY,
WHICH WILL BE GIVEN UP FOR YOU.**

The concelebrants join their hands, look toward the consecrated host as it is shown, and after this bow profoundly.

5. After this, the principal celebrant and all concelebrants continue:

**In a similar way, when supper was ended,
he took the chalice, gave you thanks
and gave the chalice to his disciples, saying:**

Each concelebrant extends his right hand toward the chalice, if this seems appropriate.

**TAKE THIS, ALL OF YOU, AND DRINK FROM IT,
FOR THIS IS THE CHALICE OF MY BLOOD,
THE BLOOD OF THE NEW AND ETERNAL COVENANT,
WHICH WILL BE POURED OUT FOR YOU AND FOR MANY
FOR THE FORGIVENESS OF SINS.**

DO THIS IN MEMORY OF ME.

The concelebrants join their hands, look toward the chalice as it is shown, and after this bow profoundly.

6. Then the principal celebrant says:

The mystery of faith.

And the concelebrants with the people continue, acclaiming:

We proclaim your Death, O Lord,
and profess your Resurrection
until you come again.

Or:

When we eat this Bread and drink this Cup,
we proclaim your Death, O Lord,
until you come again.

Or:

Save us, Savior of the world,
for by your Cross and Resurrection
you have set us free.

7. Then the principal celebrant and the concelebrants, with hands extended, say:

**Therefore, holy Father,
as we celebrate the memorial of Christ your Son,
our Savior,
whom you led through his Passion and Death on the Cross
to the glory of the Resurrection,
and whom you have seated at your right hand,
we proclaim the work of your love until he comes again
and we offer you the Bread of life
and the Chalice of blessing.**

**Look with favor on the oblation of your Church,
in which we show forth
the paschal Sacrifice of Christ that has been handed on to us,
and grant that, by the power of the Spirit of your love,
we may be counted now and until the day of eternity
among the members of your Son,
in whose Body and Blood we have communion.**

They join their hands.

With hands extended, one of the concelebrants or the principal celebrant says:

**And so, having called us to your table, Lord,
confirm us in unity,
so that, together with N. our Pope and N. our Bishop,***
**with all Bishops, Priests and Deacons,
and your entire people,
as we walk your ways with faith and hope,
we may strive to bring joy and trust into the world.**

He joins his hands.

---

* Mention may be made here of the Coadjutor Bishop, or Auxiliary Bishops, as noted in the *General Instruction of the Roman Missal*, no. 149.

With hands extended, another of the concelebrants or the principal celebrant says:

Remember our brothers and sisters (N. and N.),
who have fallen asleep in the peace of your Christ,
and all the dead, whose faith you alone have known.
Admit them to rejoice in the light of your face,
and in the resurrection give them the fullness of life.

Grant also to us,
when our earthly pilgrimage is done,
that we may come to an eternal dwelling place
and live with you for ever;
there, in communion with the Blessed Virgin Mary,
Mother of God,
with the Apostles and Martyrs,
(with Saint N.: the Saint of the day or Patron)
and with all the Saints,
we shall praise and exalt you

He joins his hands.

through Jesus Christ, your Son.

8. The principal celebrant raises the paten with the host, and the deacon, or in his absence, one of the concelebrants, raises the chalice, while the principal celebrant alone, or with all the concelebrants, says:

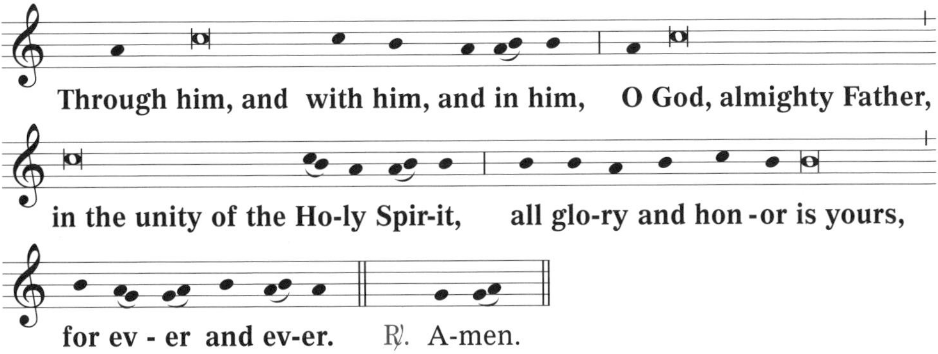
Through him, and with him, and in him, O God, almighty Father,
in the unity of the Ho-ly Spir-it, all glo-ry and hon -or is yours,
for ev - er and ev-er. ℟. A-men.

Through him, and with him, and in him,
O God, almighty Father,
in the unity of the Holy Spirit,
all glory and honor is yours,
for ever and ever.

The people acclaim:

Amen.

EUCHARISTIC PRAYER FOR USE IN MASSES FOR VARIOUS NEEDS III

Jesus, the Way to the Father

for Concelebration

The parts for all concelebrants are to be recited in a low voice and in such a way that the voice of the principal celebrant is clearly heard by the people. (See GIRM, 218.)

2. The principal celebrant, with hands extended, says:

You are indeed Holy and to be glorified, O God,
who love the human race
and who always walk with us on the journey of life.
Blessed indeed is your Son,
present in our midst
when we are gathered by his love
and when, as once for the disciples, so now for us,
he opens the Scriptures and breaks the bread.

3. The principal celebrant and all concelebrants, holding their hands extended toward the offerings, say:

Therefore, Father most merciful,
we ask that you send forth your Holy Spirit
to sanctify these gifts of bread and wine,

The principal celebrant joins his hands and makes the Sign of the Cross once over the bread and chalice together, saying:

that they may become for us
the Body and ✠ Blood

They join their hands.

of our Lord Jesus Christ.

4.

On the day before he was to suffer,
on the night of the Last Supper,
he took bread and said the blessing,
broke the bread and gave it to his disciples, saying:

Each concelebrant extends his right hand toward the bread, if this seems appropriate.

TAKE THIS, ALL OF YOU, AND EAT OF IT,
FOR THIS IS MY BODY,
WHICH WILL BE GIVEN UP FOR YOU.

The concelebrants join their hands, look toward the consecrated host as it is shown, and after this bow profoundly.

5. After this, the principal celebrant and all concelebrants continue:

In a similar way, when supper was ended,
he took the chalice, gave you thanks
and gave the chalice to his disciples, saying:

Each concelebrant extends his right hand toward the chalice, if this seems appropriate.

TAKE THIS, ALL OF YOU, AND DRINK FROM IT,
FOR THIS IS THE CHALICE OF MY BLOOD,
THE BLOOD OF THE NEW AND ETERNAL COVENANT,
WHICH WILL BE POURED OUT FOR YOU AND FOR MANY
FOR THE FORGIVENESS OF SINS.

DO THIS IN MEMORY OF ME.

The concelebrants join their hands, look toward the chalice as it is shown, and after this bow profoundly.

6. Then the principal celebrant says:

The mystery of faith.

And the concelebrants with the people continue, acclaiming:

We proclaim your Death, O Lord,
and profess your Resurrection
until you come again.

Or:

When we eat this Bread and drink this Cup,
we proclaim your Death, O Lord,
until you come again.

Or:

Save us, Savior of the world,
for by your Cross and Resurrection
you have set us free.

7. Then the principal celebrant and the concelebrants, with hands extended, say:

**Therefore, holy Father,
as we celebrate the memorial of Christ your Son,
our Savior,
whom you led through his Passion and Death on the Cross
to the glory of the Resurrection,
and whom you have seated at your right hand,
we proclaim the work of your love until he comes again
and we offer you the Bread of life
and the Chalice of blessing.**

**Look with favor on the oblation of your Church,
in which we show forth
the paschal Sacrifice of Christ that has been handed on to us,
and grant that, by the power of the Spirit of your love,
we may be counted now and until the day of eternity
among the members of your Son,
in whose Body and Blood we have communion.**

They join their hands.

With hands extended, one of the concelebrants or the principal celebrant says:

**By our partaking of this mystery, almighty Father,
give us life through your Spirit,
grant that we may be conformed to the image of your Son,
and confirm us in the bond of communion,
together with N. our Pope and N. our Bishop,*
with all other Bishops,
with Priests and Deacons,
and with your entire people.**

**Grant that all the faithful of the Church,
looking into the signs of the times by the light of faith,
may constantly devote themselves
to the service of the Gospel.**

---

* Mention may be made here of the Coadjutor Bishop, or Auxiliary Bishops, as noted in the *General Instruction of the Roman Missal*, no. 149.

Keep us attentive to the needs of all
that, sharing their grief and pain,
their joy and hope,
we may faithfully bring them the good news of salvation
and go forward with them
along the way of your Kingdom.

He joins his hands.

With hands extended, another of the concelebrants or the principal celebrant says:

Remember our brothers and sisters (N. and N.),
who have fallen asleep in the peace of your Christ,
and all the dead, whose faith you alone have known.
Admit them to rejoice in the light of your face,
and in the resurrection give them the fullness of life.

Grant also to us,
when our earthly pilgrimage is done,
that we may come to an eternal dwelling place
and live with you for ever;
there, in communion with the Blessed Virgin Mary,
Mother of God,
with the Apostles and Martyrs,
(with Saint N.: the Saint of the day or Patron**)**
and with all the Saints,
we shall praise and exalt you

He joins his hands.

through Jesus Christ, your Son.

8. The principal celebrant raises the paten with the host, and the deacon, or in his absence, one of the concelebrants, raises the chalice, while the principal celebrant alone, or with all the concelebrants, says:

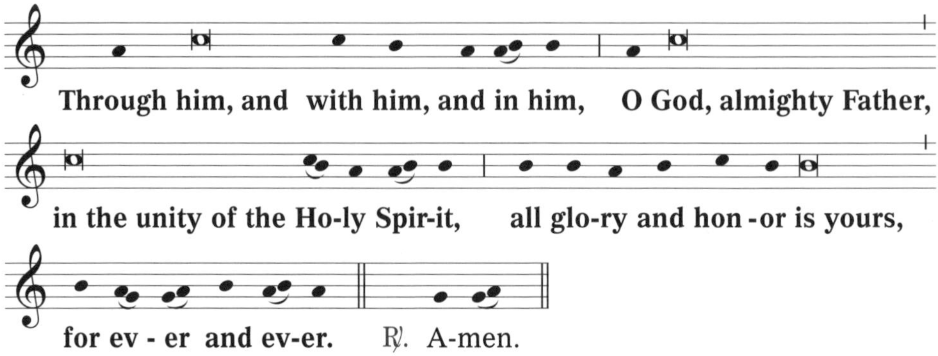
Through him, and with him, and in him, O God, almighty Father,
in the unity of the Ho-ly Spir-it, all glo-ry and hon -or is yours,
for ev - er and ev-er. ℟. A-men.

Through him, and with him, and in him,
O God, almighty Father,
in the unity of the Holy Spirit,
all glory and honor is yours,
for ever and ever.

The people acclaim:

Amen.

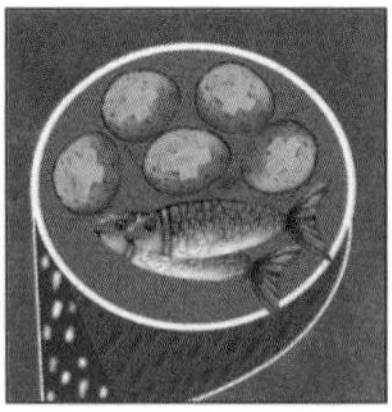

EUCHARISTIC PRAYER FOR USE IN MASSES FOR VARIOUS NEEDS IV

Jesus, Who Went About Doing Good

for Concelebration

The parts for all concelebrants are to be recited in a low voice and in such a way that the voice of the principal celebrant is clearly heard by the people. (See GIRM, 218.)

2. The principal celebrant, with hands extended, says:

You are indeed Holy and to be glorified, O God,
who love the human race
and who always walk with us on the journey of life.
Blessed indeed is your Son,
present in our midst
when we are gathered by his love
and when, as once for the disciples, so now for us,
he opens the Scriptures and breaks the bread.

3. The principal celebrant and all concelebrants, holding their hands extended toward the offerings, say:

Therefore, Father most merciful,
we ask that you send forth your Holy Spirit
to sanctify these gifts of bread and wine,

The principal celebrant joins his hands and makes the Sign of the Cross once over the bread and chalice together, saying:

that they may become for us
the Body and ✠ Blood

They join their hands.

of our Lord Jesus Christ.

4.

On the day before he was to suffer,
on the night of the Last Supper,
he took bread and said the blessing,
broke the bread and gave it to his disciples, saying:

Each concelebrant extends his right hand toward the bread, if this seems appropriate.

TAKE THIS, ALL OF YOU, AND EAT OF IT,
FOR THIS IS MY BODY,
WHICH WILL BE GIVEN UP FOR YOU.

The concelebrants join their hands, look toward the consecrated host as it is shown, and after this bow profoundly.

5. After this, the principal celebrant and all concelebrants continue:

In a similar way, when supper was ended,
he took the chalice, gave you thanks
and gave the chalice to his disciples, saying:

Each concelebrant extends his right hand toward the chalice, if this seems appropriate.

TAKE THIS, ALL OF YOU, AND DRINK FROM IT,

FOR THIS IS THE CHALICE OF MY BLOOD,

THE BLOOD OF THE NEW AND ETERNAL COVENANT,

WHICH WILL BE POURED OUT FOR YOU AND FOR MANY

FOR THE FORGIVENESS OF SINS.

DO THIS IN MEMORY OF ME.

The concelebrants join their hands, look toward the chalice as it is shown, and after this bow profoundly.

6. Then the principal celebrant says:

The mystery of faith.

And the concelebrants with the people continue, acclaiming:

We proclaim your Death, O Lord,
and profess your Resurrection
until you come again.

Or:

When we eat this Bread and drink this Cup,
we proclaim your Death, O Lord,
until you come again.

Or:

Save us, Savior of the world,
for by your Cross and Resurrection
you have set us free.

7. Then the principal celebrant and the concelebrants, with hands extended, say:

Therefore, holy Father,
as we celebrate the memorial of Christ your Son,
our Savior,
whom you led through his Passion and Death on the Cross
to the glory of the Resurrection,
and whom you have seated at your right hand,
we proclaim the work of your love until he comes again
and we offer you the Bread of life
and the Chalice of blessing.

Look with favor on the oblation of your Church,
in which we show forth
the paschal Sacrifice of Christ that has been handed on to us,
and grant that, by the power of the Spirit of your love,
we may be counted now and until the day of eternity
among the members of your Son,
in whose Body and Blood we have communion.

They join their hands.

With hands extended, one of the concelebrants or the principal celebrant says:

Bring your Church, O Lord,
to perfect faith and charity,
together with N. **our Pope and** N. **our Bishop,***
with all Bishops, Priests and Deacons,
and the entire people you have made your own.

Open our eyes
to the needs of our brothers and sisters;
inspire in us words and actions
to comfort those who labor and are burdened.
Make us serve them truly,
after the example of Christ and at his command.
And may your Church stand as a living witness
to truth and freedom,
to peace and justice,
that all people may be raised up to a new hope.

He joins his hands.

---

* Mention may be made here of the Coadjutor Bishop, or Auxiliary Bishops, as noted in the *General Instruction of the Roman Missal*, no. 149.

With hands extended, another of the concelebrants or the principal celebrant says:

Remember our brothers and sisters (N. and N.),
who have fallen asleep in the peace of your Christ,
and all the dead, whose faith you alone have known.
Admit them to rejoice in the light of your face,
and in the resurrection give them the fullness of life.

Grant also to us,
when our earthly pilgrimage is done,
that we may come to an eternal dwelling place
and live with you for ever;
there, in communion with the Blessed Virgin Mary,
Mother of God,
with the Apostles and Martyrs,
(with Saint N.: the Saint of the day or Patron**)**
and with all the Saints,
we shall praise and exalt you

He joins his hands.

through Jesus Christ, your Son.

8. The principal celebrant raises the paten with the host, and the deacon, or in his absence, one of the concelebrants, raises the chalice, while the principal celebrant alone, or with all the concelebrants, says:

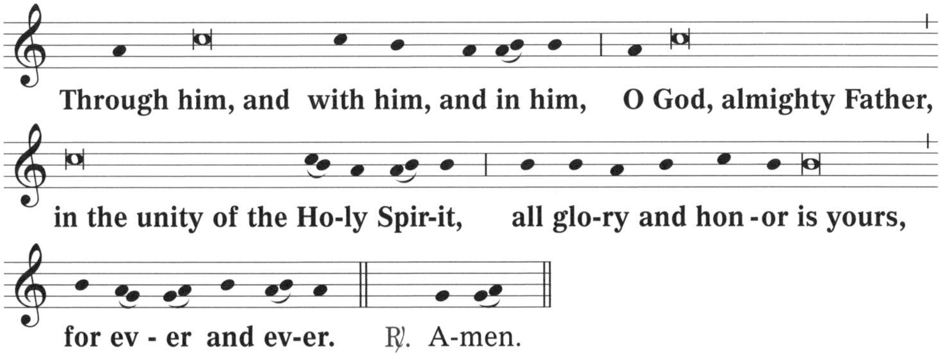
Through him, and with him, and in him, O God, almighty Father,
in the unity of the Ho-ly Spir-it, all glo-ry and hon-or is yours,
for ev - er and ev-er. ℟. A-men.

Through him, and with him, and in him,
O God, almighty Father,
in the unity of the Holy Spirit,
all glory and honor is yours,
for ever and ever.

The people acclaim:

Amen.

THE APOSTLES' CREED

Instead of the Niceno-Constantinopolitan Creed, especially during Lent and Easter Time, the baptismal Symbol of the Roman Church, known as the Apostles' Creed, may be used.

I believe in God,
the Father almighty,
Creator of heaven and earth,
and in Jesus Christ, his only Son, our Lord,

At the words that follow, up to and including the Virgin Mary, *all bow.*

who was conceived by the Holy Spirit,
born of the Virgin Mary,
suffered under Pontius Pilate,
was crucified, died and was buried;
he descended into hell;
on the third day he rose again from the dead;
he ascended into heaven,
and is seated at the right hand of God the Father almighty;
from there he will come to judge the living and the dead.

I believe in the Holy Spirit,
the holy catholic Church,
the communion of saints,
the forgiveness of sins,
the resurrection of the body,
and life everlasting. Amen.